IMAGES
of England

CHESTERTON

The centre of the village of (Old) Chesterton is seen in this aerial view of 1996. On the left is the River Cam crossed by the Green Dragon footbridge from Water Street. Left of centre Water Lane runs to the High Street which passes through the centre of the village to the Hall at top right. The recreation ground is to the left of the Hall, then the parish church of St Andrew. The Pye/Philips/Simoco factories dominate the top left with their playing fields beside the river. Above the factories is the Elizabeth Way bridge, which opened in 1971. The square building opposite Water Lane is the Cambridge City Council's residential home for the elderly, Whitefriars. Below it, Green End Road curves round to the octagonal Methodist church and onto the Ely Road. Scotland Road is on the right of the picture. (Picture courtesy of *Cambridge Evening News*)

IMAGES
of England

CHESTERTON

Compiled by
Chesterton Local History Group

Anne Bromley
Alice Zeitlyn
Christine Gibson
Brian Woods
John Norman
Colin Moule
Derek Stubbings

TEMPUS

First published 2000
Copyright © Chesterton Local History Group, 2000

Tempus Publishing Limited
The Mill, Brimscombe Port,
Stroud, Gloucestershire, GL5 2QG

ISBN 0 7524 1861 0

Typesetting and origination by
Tempus Publishing Limited
Printed in Great Britain by
Midway Clark Printing, Wiltshire

Contents

Young members of the Chesterton Chapel string band, *c.* 1888 (see p. 50).

Foreword

I am delighted to welcome this latest addition to the story of Cambridge and its area. Chesterton is now to many eyes just a suburb of Cambridge, but to many who live there, it has its own separate community. It has its own story, its own characters and its own character. Like everywhere else, Chesterton has undergone changes, some of which are to be welcomed, others regretted. A book of photographs such as this records just how the area used to look, its buildings, streetscapes, and people, at a precise moment in history.

While the photographer has captured a moment in time, the captions written by those who know and love the area add even more – giving an insight into conditions, the way of life and the essential feeling of the place.

Together these words and pictures present a vivid portrait of a way of life which has disappeared. As well as presenting Chestertonians with a marvellous feast of memories and nostalgia, it gives the researcher of the future a most valuable source of information about life in this area of Cambridge through the twentieth century.

Mike Petty MBE
Researcher, writer and lecturer on Cambridgeshire and the Fens

Mr Fieldgate, landlord of the Maltsters Arms, with his young family, c. 1904 (see p. 85).

Introduction

Although there is evidence of occupation in Chesterton before Roman times, the Roman agricultural area of Arbury (although not part of this archive) gave the village its name, meaning 'The farm by the castle.'

By Norman times the famous Stourbridge Fair was almost certainly established and, although it was just across the River Cam in the Cambridge suburb of Barnwell, its influence on Chesterton was, for several hundred years, enormous.

The village itself fitted compactly into the South East corner of the parish and was largely agricultural, but with some influence from the trade passing along the river.

For some 230 years, from 1217, the village was owned and administered by the Abbey of Vercelli in Italy. Chesterton Towers, in the heart of the village, remains the only visible reminder of that time.

The village was enclosed in 1840 and development of the western area, known as New Chesterton, quickly followed. Still a civil parish, the whole area was absorbed into Cambridge in 1912.

Old Chesterton slowly developed in the 1920s and 1930s, but after 1945 expansion was rapid, both in the Arbury area and in the village itself.

Acknowledgements

Our thanks are due to:
Cambridegshire Collection
Cambridge and County Folk Museum
Cambridge Evening News
Chesterton Challenge
Roy's Leisure
Two Tees Boatyard
Mrs P. Marsh
Lesley and Derek Flory
Mrs B. Hogg
Mrs S. Hogg
F.H. Stanford

Other photographs were supplied by members of the Local History Group.

The authors have made every effort to ensure that the information contained in these pages is as full and as accurate as possible but would be pleased to hear from any readers who may be able to add to the information provided.

One
The River Cam

The Green Dragon pub and the ferry seen from the towpath on Stourbridge Common, *c.* 1879.

View of Chesterton in 1838 from Castle Hill, the Western boundary of the parish. The Ely road curves away on the left, passing the Spring Brewery. In the centre is the site of Dant's ferry

crossing with Chesterton parish church on the horizon.

Strange's boathouse, nestled at the foot of the Victoria Gardens embankment, provided punts and other craft. A few yards downstream was Jesus Lock which discouraged use of the lower river. Upstream were other boathouses, better placed for The Backs. Consequently, Strange's was never much used and disappeared long ago.

Jesus Green Lock in 1879, showing the early low level footbridge and cock-up bridge over the lock. The lock keeper's residence was a single-storey building. Jesus Green is low lying and quickly floods after heavy rain or snowfall.

Jesus Lock in 1890 when the keeper's house had been enlarged to two storeys. The unmade bank and shallow water was then ideal for youngsters to use.

In the early 1900s the footbridge at Jesus Lock was becoming much used as New Chesterton was developed and the Cambridge Instrument Company became established. The whole footbridge was then replaced by a one-level structure.

Pleasure trips on the Cam were very popular. The steam launch *Otter*, here at Jesus Lock around 1896, hosts an outing of the Licensed Victuallers' Association.

On the bank of the Cam in Chesterton Road between Jesus Lock and Victoria Bridge was the Spring Brewery, pictured around 1900.

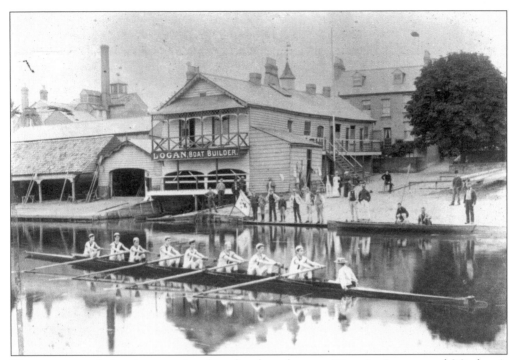

The area around the river crossing (at what later became Victoria Avenue and Mitcham's Corner) built up as shops were established along the road and boatyards along the river bank. This scene in 1885 is of Logan's boathouse, with a college crew posing in their eight. Spring Brewery over the boat sheds is on the left.

Thought to be the official 1890 picture of the bridge on the new Victoria Avenue across Midsummer Common. The ferry, soon to be taken out of use, is tied up on the Chesterton bank. Logan's boatyard is seen under the bridge.

The long-awaited Victoria Avenue and bridge over the Cam attracted huge crowds at the official opening on 11 December 1890.

The college boat clubs built their boathouses from the Victoria Bridge along the river bank towards Chesterton. That of Lady Margaret Boat Club (St John's College) sits beside the bridge facing across Midsummer Common.

William Bates on his ferry in the 1890s. The means of propulsion, wheel and chain, can clearly be seen.

The Cam from Victoria Bridge, Cambridge

POCOCK WINTER

River scenes attracted the attention of picture postcard firms. This card, by Valentines, is a view from Victoria Avenue bridge downstream, showing boathouses and a variety of pleasure craft.

The Fort St George public house originally stood on an island in the river. A ferry of early, but unknown, date provided a crossing from Chesterton to Midsummer Common via the pub. The footpath from Chesterton Road became Ferry Path and provided a picturesque crossing point before the area was built up.

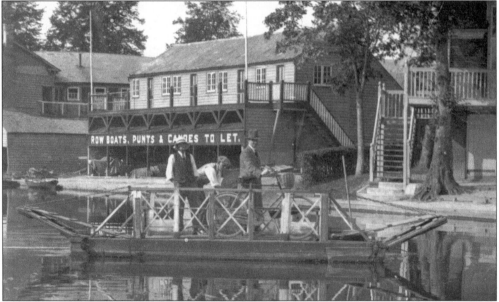

The Fort St George ferry, as it became known, was probably the busiest of all, running from 8 a.m. to 10 p.m. In the 1920s the fare was a halfpenny each way. The ferry was replaced by a footbridge in 1927.

The college boathouses vary considerably in style. Contrast Caius boathouse with that of Trinity Hall.

Trinity Hall boathouse with T. Foster's University boathouse adjoining.

Another much-used ferry. Again in rather rural surroundings, was Dant's Ferry. A footpath from Cam Road (now part of Elizabeth Way) led between boathouses to the cottage in which Mr Dant lived. He had owned and operated in earlier years a steam tug and a string of barges. The ferry gave access to the Cambridge bank and to Newmarket Road. It was often called Dant's Ferry, being used by a large number of the workforce at the new and expanding Pye Radio works in St Andrew's Road, Chesterton.

A more modern picture, from the 1950s, of the footbridge which replaced Dant's Ferry, seen from the vantage point of one of Banham's holiday cruisers.

Banham Marina. The boatbuilding firm of H.C. Banham had existed for many years, making craft for the college boat clubs as well as their own fleet of holiday cruisers. The new river crossing of Elizabeth Way went through the middle of the site. A new building was erected on part of the site and boatbuilding continued for a few more years but closed completely in the 1970s. The scene in 1970 has the new bridge under construction on the right with the *Viscountess Bury* (with lifebelts) below it.

The *Viscountess Bury* is one of the best known pleasure boats on the river. Owned and operated on the Cam for many years by Banham's, it has since undergone a complete restoration. It was built in 1888 as a pioneering electrically-driven boat and was used on the Thames by Edward VII.

This scene dates back only twenty-five years, but now looks very different. The river bank is now fully made up, backed by shrubs and small trees, the meadow is fronted by a 'pocket' nature park, and the rest occupied by a large residential home.

The river crossing at Chesterton was known as the Horse Grind or the Green Dragon pub ferry. The ferry existed for many hundreds of years. It served the world-famous Stourbridge Fair and was the only crossing point for horse-drawn vehicles apart from Magdalene Bridge in Cambridge and, later, Victoria Avenue. The ferry was replaced in 1937 by a footbridge which served the large number of people from the expanding Barnwell area across the river who cycled or walked to work at the growing Pye Radio or Cambridge Instrument Company works in Chesterton.

Time of change. Piles being driven for the erection of the new bridge to replace the Green Dragon ferry in 1937.

In the heyday of the Stourbridge Fair, the Green Dragon ferry was in continual use and then the two ferries would be lined up to act as a form of bridge as shown in this scene.

The Green Dragon passenger ferry on the Barnwell bank. On Stourbridge Common can be seen the once famous international fair. Here, on a September day in the late 1920s, it is much reduced and in fact closed for good in 1932. This is the only known photograph of the fair.

A Valentine postcard of the Pike and Eel public house as it was seen from Stourbridge Common around the 1920s. Behind the boats on the water is the large ferry, while the small ferry approaches those waiting on the Barnwell bank.

AFTER THE RACES.

The finishing post for the rowing races is by the riverside pub, the Pike and Eel, which was also the terminus for special bus services from Cambridge in the 1920s and '30s. Many spectators went by boat downstream to moor against the banks along the racecourse. After the last race they returned upstream to Cambridge, often in impromptu races themselves. Here is a cartoonist's picture of the scene at the Pike and Eel.

Until 1834, the Pike and Eel in Water Street stood beside a lock. The lockside is the open space in this picture. The towpath from Kings Lynn reached Chesterton here and the ferry in the pub grounds took it on to the Barnwell bank to continue along Stourbridge Common in Cambridge and Quayside.

The railway came to Cambridge in 1845 and continued on to Kings Lynn, crossing the Cam on the outskirts of Chesterton via a trestle bridge, later replaced by a low girder bridge – seen here awaiting removal in 1930 when a much larger and stronger bridge was built. The work was carried out over a weekend and attracted large crowds of sightseers. The signals controlled the junction of the St Ives branch line.

Lone symbol of the importance of Chesterton Junction was the signal box, now gone, which could just be seen from the river.

Two
The High Street

Chesterton High Street provided many interesting views for local photographers, such as this scene in 1913. The thatched cottages are visible and Arthur's Buildings can be glimpsed on the right past the shop.

The Hall, until development spread out from Cambridge, was the first building in Chesterton. Dating from the early seventeenth century, it was built of red brick when brickwork was becoming popular for buildings of this type. It was remodelled extensively in the mid-nineteenth century and enlarged after 1900. It has since been converted into Cambridge City Council flats.

Among the later remodelling of the Hall was the removal of the coachhouse to another part of the estate. The construction of Elizabeth Way in the 1970s separated the coachhouse and other buildings from the main Hall with a large traffic island. The coachhouse and grounds now contain a large residential block and disabled people's workshops.

Chesterton Road, before Elizabeth Way was built, went past the front of the Hall. At the back was a meadow, in this picture, before surrounding properties were demolished and the road re-aligned.

Among the demolished properties was a row of Victorian cottages (Barleycorn Lane) off the High Street, approached by a wide passageway on one side of the meadow.

At the entrance to the village facing the High Street was a line of Victorian cottages. The High Wall opposite surrounded (and still does) the garden of Chesterton House.

The High Street cottages were demolished to allow for the road re-alignment, leaving a view of the gable end of the former Bowling Green public house.

The former Bowling Green public house, dating from 1789, now offices. With several names over the years, it took this name from the bowling green laid out in the back garden.

Opposite the Bowling Green, a row of cottages contained a newsagents and a pub, the Prince Albert. These have all been replaced by new houses.

A large house of varying dates and building additions stands on the High Street corner of Chapel Street. Largely timber-framed and now brick-faced, it deteriorated into a poor condition. Restoration took several years, but eventually provided an attractive and interesting building in the street scene.

A pair of clay and clunch thatched cottages stood on a bend in the High Street until demolished in the early 1930s to be replaced by a terrace of four houses.

Next to the thatched cottages was a distinctive row of houses known as Arthur's Buildings. Cleared in the 1950s, they were replaced by a group of flats for council tenants.

Living in Arthur's Buildings was Stephen Wilson. He kept a greengrocer's shop there, for which he grew much of his produce on a nearby allotment and a smallholding in Arbury Road. A horse and cart provided the means, until 1948, of selling his produce in the village.

Many Victorian cottages in the High Street were demolished in the 1950s and 1960s to be replaced by new houses. Some had already gone when this bus misjudged the sharp bend and assisted with further demolition!

The High Street (to the right) at its junction with Church Street.

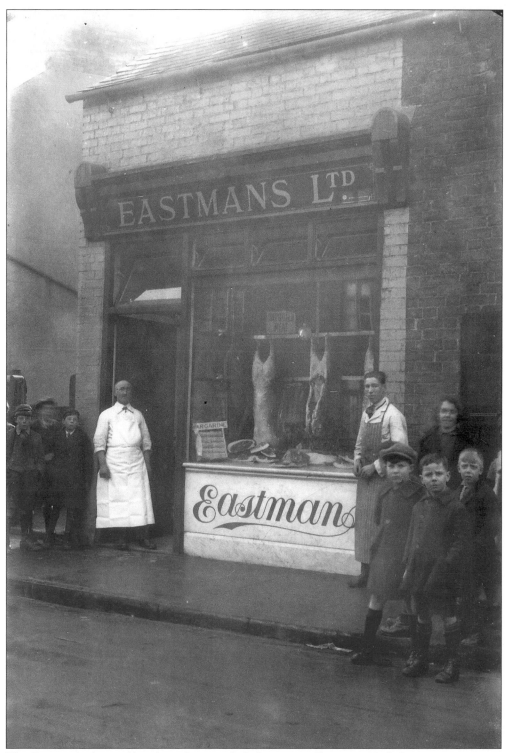

The Eastman's chain of butchers shops included many small ones in High Street situations, such as this one in the 1920s.

The Dog and Pheasant public house remains almost unaltered since this postcard was issued in the late 1920s. The row of houses was built on the site of various yards behind advertisement hoardings, and set well back for road widening which never took place.

This 1963 view of the High Street was captured before many of the houses were cleared. The Impey family, whose name appears over the shop, were well-known bakers in the village.

The same stretch of High Street as in the previous picture but seen at the other end, by Ferry Lane, in the early 1920s. The corner shop had a succession of uses, including a greengrocer and Salvation Army coffee rooms.

The High Street, looking towards Green End Road, in the early 1920s. The building on the left is the British Queen public house. It was demolished in the 1950s and the ground used for temporary classrooms for the nearby St Andrew's School.

These cottages in the High Street and Green End Road date from the mid-nineteenth century and were demolished in the early 1950s to be replaced by Cambridge City Council's Whitefriars home for the elderly.

The postmaster, Mr Frank Bailey, and his family outside Chesterton Post Office in the 1920s. His son, John, later became postmaster, the third generation to do so.

Three
Churches and Schools

Old Chesterton Church.

The parish church of St Andrew, in a rural setting in the first few years of the twentieth century. The footpath from Haig Road crossed the recreation ground and through the churchyard. To the right of the church is the Old Manor House.

St Andrew's church, around 100 years ago. The cottage on the left survived until the 1950s as did the Manor House, the end of which is on the right.

St. Andrew's Church, Chesterton

One of the famous Valentines postcards. The church in the early 1900s, when the road had been made up and the rustic gates in the last picture replaced by a new gate with cast-iron posts to the footpath.

At the beginning of the twentieth century the village was increasing in population and the need for extra land in the churchyard was urgent. On 19 July 1912 the Bishop of Ely consecrated the additional land. These are two of a set of pictures taken by a local photographer.

St Andrew's Church Chesterton.
Consecration of Additional Land
July 19th 1912.

Demolition of old cottages in Water Street in the 1930s revealed the threshold of one cottage to be the base of a village cross, which was taken to the churchyard for preservation. The cottages faced a small green which could possibly have been a small market.

The parish church of St Andrew is well known for its many and varied pew ends. This mediaeval gentleman faces his companion across the aisle.

The church has a fine, but incomplete, Doom painting over the chancel arch. It has been restored and fully interpreted. The East window was donated by a well-known butcher, Mr Samuel Rickard, to celebrate the diamond jubilee of Queen Victoria.

The church had a strong following of young people, including the Church Lads' Brigade, who won the Lucas-Tooth Shield seen here, about which, unfortunately, little is known.

Over the years the church choir and members of the congregation put on many dramatic productions in the church hall. Those from 1935 and 1938 are shown here.

The Boys' Brigade was always very strong in Cambridge, the Chesterton 4th Company having been started in association with the company at Christchurch in Barnwell. The Chesterton company are here at the back of the Boys' School in the High Street around 1910.

The Wesleyan Methodists opened their new chapel in the High Street in 1858 and it was used until sold in 1904, when they moved to a newly-built chapel in Church Street. This was in the grounds of Meadowcroft, owned by Mr B.A. Jolley, one of their members. The original chapel building became the home of the Chesterton Men's Club, as pictured here.

The 1904 Methodist chapel is an attractive building, the entrance to which is seen here. It was bought by Pyes in 1942 for their own use, the Methodists moving to new premises in Green End Road.

The growing district of New Chesterton had a Congregational church opened in Victoria Road in 1884 with extensions in 1899. It was demolished in 1989 to be replaced by housing society accommodation and the nearby St Luke's church was refurbished to provide facilities for both the church and the United Reformed church, as the Congregationalists had become known.

As the new areas of Chesterton developed along Milton Road, a new parish of St George's was formed. Temporary premises in Chesterfield Road served from 1931 until the new church was completed in 1938.

The church of St George's is an impressive building with a prominent south west tower.

New Chesterton was the first new parish created out of St Andrew's. A temporary wooden church was provided in 1863 for the new church of St Luke's and a completely new building was consecrated in 1874, to be completed in 1885 and seating 770.

The Chesterton Band of Hope seen, probably, in the vicarage ground, around 1900.

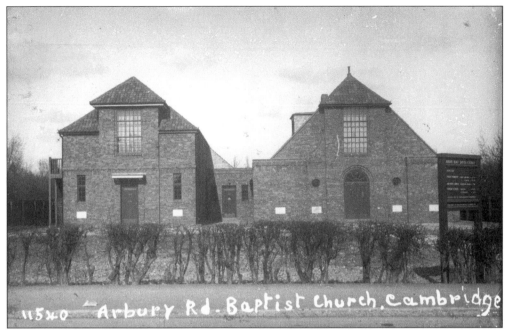

Baptists had been active in Chesterton for many years and in 1842 built a substantial chapel in local brick in Chapel Street. It was extended in 1863 to seat about 450 people. The building was sold in 1930 to become the hall for the parish church of St Andrew and the Baptists moved to a new church in Arbury Road.

The Baptist church Sunday school teachers in 1900.

The string band of the Baptist church around 1888.

Chapel Sunday school teachers and friends, 1896.

The National School opened in 1844 on land in Town Close bought from the Parish Charity and was used until demolished in 1969. A new and larger school building was erected in 1870 and was much enlarged to cater for the growing numbers of school children. The senior children moved in 1935 to the new Chesterton Secondary School in Gilbert Road and the infants went to the new Shirley School in Green End Road in 1932. St Andrew's remained a junior mixed school until completely demolished in 1985 after the new St Andrew's opened in Nuffield Road in 1982.

The National School building of 1844, photographed sometime in the 1920s.

St Andrew's School mixed class of 1913 – Group 1.

St Andrew's School boys' class of 1913 – Group 9.

St Andrew's School mixed class of 1913 – Group 2.

St Andrew's School girls' class of 1913 – Group 10.

St Andrew's School girls' class, probably 1913. The teacher is Miss M. Hunneybun.

The Chesterton Preparatory School in De Freville Avenue was housed in its own building in pleasant grounds. Founded in 1910, it took both infants and juniors. In the summer, classes held in the garden were popular with the children.

The Chesterton Preparatory School making full use of its attractive grounds near the river.

The Preparatory School held an annual sports day when parents were especially welcome. A display of maypole dancing was always popular.

In 1908 the county council opened the first non-church school in Chesterton at the junction of Milton Road and Gilbert Road. It provided both infant and junior schools.

Increasing numbers of children and additional subjects taught often meant using other buildings. This former coachhouse and stable of Roebuck House in Water Street was used for some time as the woodwork classroom for boys at St Andrew's School.

Four
Housing in the Village

Chesterton Tower is some 600 years old. Standing in the former vicarage gardens, it is a two-storey building. In 1217 the village was presented by King Henry III to a Papal Legate in recognition of assistance in keeping peace in this country. It was then transferred to the care of the Abbey of Vercelli in Italy. Reclaimed in 1444, it eventually came into the possession of Trinity College. This print of the tower is from around 1888 when it was being used as a barn.

The junction of High Street and Church Street, looking towards Chapel Street. On the left is Webb's Bakery.

Number 22, Church Street, a fine Victorian House, built *c.* 1838.

Church Street as seen from Chapel Street junction, looking towards the High Street. The row of houses on the right is Pye Terrace with a date stone of 1901.

The entrance door to 22 Church Street with a cast iron framed, semi-circular window over it.

The former vicarage, now a private house, dating from *c.* 1820. It stands in its own grounds, a short walk from the church.

The coachhouse and stables to the former vicarage, almost unchanged since being built in about 1820.

The Manor House, built in the late seventeenth century, stood facing the church in its own extensive grounds. It was red brick, later refaced, with an added west wing and had an unusual but attractive two-storey brick summer house in the garden. Demolished in 1971, the site was developed and is now occupied by old people's flats.

A pair of cottages. Manor Cottages, in Church Street.

Chesterton House in Church Street is a large property in its own grounds. It was built in the late eighteenth century but has been much extended and altered over the years.

The garden front of Chesterton House.

The eighteenth-century pigeon house in the grounds of Chesterton House. The nesting boxes have since gone.

This is known as the Old Manor House, just South of St Andrew's church. It is a two-storey building, plastered with timber-framed walls and was built about 1700. It has been extended and modernised and is now used for offices.

Number 6, Chapel Street, built *c.* 1880.

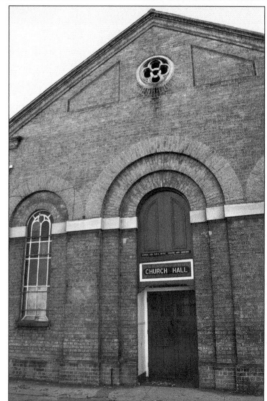

The former Baptist chapel in Church Street, built in 1842 and extended in 1863. It has a three-bay front and windows under rounded arcading. The Baptists moved to a new church in Arbury Road and the chapel was sold in 1930 to become the church hall for St Andrew's.

Chesterton Tower today is much restored but still retains its appearance and now serves as offices.

During the Second World War the church hall served as a British Restaurant and was the scene of a victory party (seen here) in 1945.

Scotland Road in the early 1920s as seen from Green End Road.

By the latter half of the 1920s, Scotland Road had become part of a council housing estate, with a small shop at the Green End Road corner.

This early Victorian cottage was part of the rural Scotland Road. It still survives today.

Sand and gravel digging had been a prominent local industry for many years. Although only shallow diggings, they were usually dry. One of the last excavations is shown here on the recreation ground near the church in 1932. Pye's factory is in the background.

This attractive house accommodated Murrell's Nurseries in Scotland Road in 1922, but was soon to be replaced by council houses.

The nurseries had several greenhouses producing mainly salad, vegtables and flowers for the local market.

This view taken from upper windows of Scotland Farm house in the early 1920s has Murrell's Nursery on the left and, on the extreme right, St Andrew's School can be seen through the trees.

Scotland Farm stood at the Union Lane end of Scotland Road. A large farmhouse, with the substantial barns and outbuildings of an active farm, it gradually gave way to sporadic sand and gravel digging prior to and during the Second World War.

The farmhouse faced towards Union Lane over an attractive garden enclosed by a high wall.

Roebuck House is a substantial early eighteenth-century property in Water Street, rebuilt in 1775, partly brick and partly timber. The gardens face down towards the river and across Stourbridge Common.

Parts of Roebuck House date back to the early seventeenth century as seen in this timber-framed barn.

Number 15 Water Street is timber-framed but brick fronted, of early seventeenth-century origin but much altered and extended.

Water Street in this view of 1930 was a street entirely made up of seventeenth- and eighteenth-century cottages with, behind them, several rows of squalid, mean cottages.

Most of the Water Street cottages had been demolished by the 1930s but these remained until 1953.

At the Fen Road end of Water Street was a small village green faced by these typical Fenland cottages, which were demolished in the 1930s to allow the Hundred Houses Society's Fallowfield estate to be built.

The Pike and Eel public house is where Water Street becomes Chesterton Fen Road. The towpath reached Chesterton through the posts on the right of the picture, beside an open space next to the pub where, until 1834, there was a lock.

Few's Corner in Water Street was, up to the 1930s, a farm. The house on the corner was converted from a barn. Another wooden barn with a corrugated roof can be seen. The whole site has been redeveloped and is now occupied by flats.

The farmhouse of Few's Farm in Water Street was demolished at the end of the Second World War. The fire mark of the Guardian Royal Exchange Company was removed for preservation.

Five
Mitcham's Corner

In the early 1900s the original Scales Hotel faces a street lamp in the centre of the very broad road junction. The direction signs read 'Cambridge' (to the left) and 'Old Chesterton' (to the right). The Great Eastern Railway booking office occupies part of the hotel. Dants, next door, are the local bakers. The view extends up Victoria Road to St Luke's church.

A busy scene at Mitcham's Corner with a view along Chesterton Road, *c.* 1912. Behind the bus, the hoardings hide the Jolly Waterman public house, still to be rebuilt. Mitcham's shop was established in 1909, selling dress-making materials, wool, and haberdashery with clothing and

other goods added later. The business was very successful, taking in adjoining shops and, with other businesses, the area became an important secondary shopping centre. Although Mitcham's closed in 1977, the name lives on as one of the busiest road junctions in Cambridge.

Until the opening of the new bridge and Victoria Avenue in 1895, a ferry operated at this point. The road from the ferry to Chesterton Road was known as Bridge Road.

All important river crossings feature a public house at or near the crossing point. The Jolly Waterman is on the main road just yards from the river crossing and remained, as in this picture, until about 1930. It was said to be the only building between Cambridge and Chesterton in 1850.

Chesterton Road is a wide road and was once lined with trees, a few of which still remain. Here, in 1925, Mitcham's shop has expanded round the corner, and is dominated by the distinctive house, part of the premises.

Looking towards Mitcham's shop, again in 1925, the houses along Chesterton Road are gradually being extended into shops.

On the corner of Trafalgar Road, G.P. Hawkins set up their new branch bakery shop in 1925, with a smart modern front. Hawkins was a well-known business, with the Dorothy Café and several bakery shops in Cambridge. Although the business closed down long ago, this shop is still a baker's.

Opposite Mitcham's shop is a row of substantial three-storey houses with basements, built at the end of the nineteenth century for successful local traders who could afford to keep staff. These houses still exist, though now in the form of bed-sit accommodation and are isolated at the centre of the busy traffic circulation system.

Many pictures of Chesterton, including Mitcham's Corner, are the work of a local photographer in the 1920s. These large houses opposite Mitcham's repeat in part other views, but here, on the left, is a building long gone which, in 1894, housed the offices of Chesterton Urban District Council. It includes a police box, outside of which can be seen a police constable.

A major road junction was an excellent situation for a petrol station and car showrooms. King and Harpers, just in Milton Road and part of Mitcham's Corner, occupied these premises when photographed in 1922 until 1966 when the site was redeveloped into offices and furniture showrooms.

Even in 1930 it was possible to photograph Mitcham's Corner without any cars. Looking down Chesterton Road, Mitcham's shop occupies the corner, facing the Jolly Waterman, soon to be rebuilt. Barclays Bank remained for much longer, but was later completely rebuilt.

From the same point as the previous photograph, but looking in the opposite direction towards Cambridge. Scales Hotel, soon to be rebuilt, partly obscures Lloyds Bank on the Victoria Road corner. The Tivoli cinema, to the left of Lloyds, is masked by trees. In the centre of this wide junction are the public toilets, now buried underground.

The Tivoli was the second purpose-built cinema in Cambridge, opening in March 1925 and replacing the Spring Brewery on the site. The cinema closed in 1956, becoming a warehouse for several years and now has a new lease of life as a large chain public house brewing much of its own beer.

Adjoining a cinema tends to be a good spot for other businesses. Next to the Tivoli was a shop, being at various times a hairdresser's and a café, but it is now all part of the public house known as the Boathouse. It was known earlier as the Rob Roy, after a prominent rowing club on the River Cam.

Typical of the wide range of shops around Mitcham's Corner serving the local population before the First World War was the shoe shop of A. Philips.

Mr G.M. Prior stands proudly with his special display of pork meat with a notice to tell customers it was home-produced.

Six
Public Houses and Inns

In a prominent position in the High Street facing on to 'The Green' stood the Maltsters Arms, landlord Mr Fieldgate. He had three daughters and a young son, all seen here gathered round the tree on the green in about 1904. In the background is Hill House.

The Fleur de Lys public house, built in Cam Road on the edge of the de Freville estate. Once a quiet urban residential road, it is now part of the Elizabeth Way inner ring road.

Patrons of the Fleur de Lys assembled for their outing in 1946.

The Haymakers, built in about 1860, stands in the High Street, facing Union Lane, as seen in the 1920s.

A social occasion in the 1920s for the patrons of the Haymakers on Chesterton recreation ground, but sadly details are unknown.

The Dog and Pheasant in the High Street has remained unaltered externally for many years.

Outside the Dog and Pheasant the Outing Club prepare to leave in the 1920s.

This is 28 August 1958 and the Dog and Pheasant patrons have their photographs taken before leaving for their outing to Southend.

The White Horse Inn in the High Street, next to Thrifts Walk, had been demolished by 1910 and replaced by a row of three houses. The landlord, Mr Brown, and his family pose outside.

Scales Hotel, a large and popular hostelry at Mitcham's Corner, on the junction of Victoria Road and Milton Road, remained until around 1930 when it was replaced by the Portland Arms. It had stables and hired out carriages. A large barn at the back was the venue for many local societies' meetings.

A very large public house, the Golden Hind opened on Coronation Day 1937 in a prominent position in Milton Road for the traveller entering Cambridge. Unusually, however, only a few photographs exist. A large group is gathered here in 1945 for the victory party to celebrate the end of the Second World War.

The Green Dragon in Water Street is housed in half of a very interesting range of timber-framed buildings. A public house has existed for several hundred years in this position. It is an important area facing the former ferries, both foot and vehicle, which existed until 1937 when replaced by a footbridge to Stourbridge Common.

The only known picture of the Yorkshire Grey public house in the High Street as it existed in 1910 and before rebuilding took place in the 1930s.

A well-known riverside pub, the Pike and Eel, here in the 1880s. This was an important position as here the towpath from Kings Lynn entered Chesterton and a ferry in the Pike and

Eel grounds continued the towpath across the river to continue into Cambridge.

Pride of place in the Cambridge and County Folk Museum is held for the silver belt won by Charles Rowell, the world champion long-distance runner. A Chesterton man, Rowell defeated the reigning champion in Madison Square Gardens in New York in 1879 and, after further successes in 1881, won the belt outright. His welcome home party was held in the Bleeding Heart public house (formerly known as the Maltster's Arms) in the High Street and kept by members of the Rowell family.

Gathered in the bar round the fire on dark winter evenings, the bargees made their own amusement at the Pike and Eel, perhaps in competition with local residents. The tallest of the tall tales would have earned this unique small medallion – The Noted Liar – now in the possession of the Cambridge and County Folk Museum.

Seven
Almshouses

The Victoria Asylum in Victoria Road was opened in 1841 by Cambridge Friendly Society for twelve respectable elderly members. The original block which had a date stone of 1838 has been demolished, as have some later bungalows. An attractive bungalow block and some modern bungalows still remain.

The Chesterton Union is a substantial workhouse built to standard pattern on the village outskirts in 1838. Built of local bricks with a slate roof, mainly three storeys in height, it contained the usual male and female wards plus a ward for vagrants and quarters for the Master and Mistress. It served thirty-three parishes to the north and west of Chesterton. To cater for families taken in, the Union had its own school with classrooms for boys and girls. With its own teachers, it was quite separate from the village school.

The staff and board of guardians of Chesterton Union in 1935.

11352 Union Lane, Cambridge

Union Lane at the High Street end had an almshouse, seen here on the right behind the woman, part of a group on the High Street. The bungalow on the left was one of a pair provided by a wealthy local resident, Mr Emily Wood. All have now been demolished. The Haymaker pub faces up Union Lane.

Almshouses facing the High Street were built c. 1860, then said to be a good example of housing for the poor and elderly. They were demolished during the Second World War to allow Hallens (the adjoining garage) to build workshops to service military vehicles.

The Mansfield almshouses in Church Street form an attractive row of four bungalows founded in 1891 for the benefit of single women living in Chesterton. Modernised in 1987, two similar bungalows were added on ground at the rear.

H. Slater, chairman of the board of management for the Victoria Homes.

Jubilee Day 1935, and the residents of Victoria Homes celebrate in front of the pavilion.

The Victoria Homes in 1937.

Staff and residents of Victoria Homes, *c.* 1920.

Eight

Pye Radio

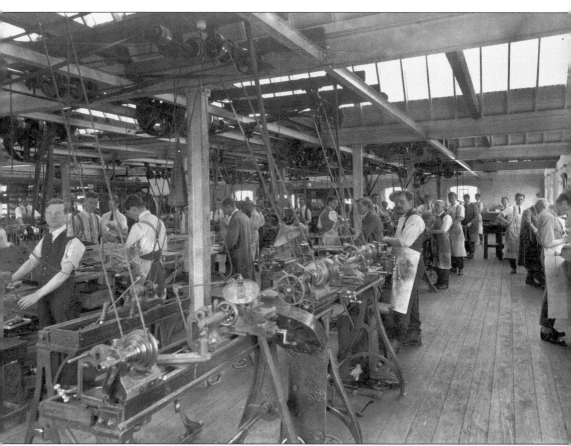

Pye Radio in the 1930s – the lathe shop. This world famous company began in a small way in Chesterton and rapidly grew to become a leading producer of radios, televisions and other domestic appliances.

Pye Radio, 1930. The offices in St Andrew's Road.

The early Pye factory and offices on the north side of St Andrew's Road faced across riverside meadows.

The machine shop at Pye Radio in the 1930s.

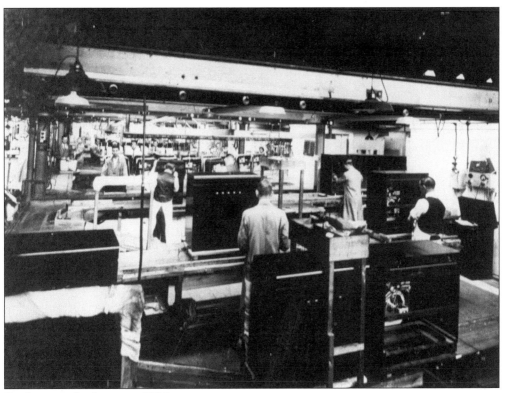

Production of radiograms, 1936.

Radio set production in the 1920s.

The assembly lines decorated for Christmas 1955. Pictured are some of the many women employees.

Always a popular event, the works outing in north bay at Cambridge station. The outing was possibly one to Great Yarmouth in 1935.

The Pye Ladies netball team in 1932.

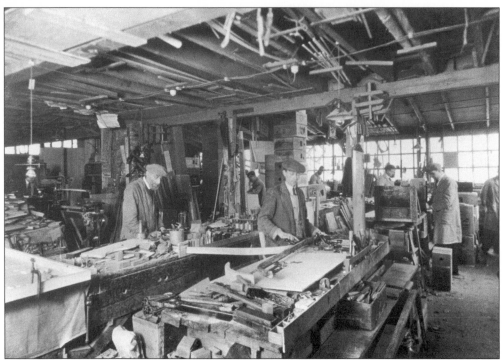

The Carters cabinet-making works in Cam Road, 1920s.

A further view of the Carters works.

Nine
Village Life

In the 1920s and 1930s the Chivers jam factory at Histon employed many people from Chesterton and East Cambridge who cycled along Arbury Road. Apart from a few houses at the Milton Road end, Arbury Road ran through farmland and orchards. At Milton Road the street nameplate, which has since disappeared, has a special wooden plate added to direct cyclists to Histon.

Victorian houses line St Luke's Street, leading to the church whose spire can be seen. The street, on the north slopes of Castle Hill, marks the first stretch of the Roman road to Ely, known locally as Mere Way. The course of this Roman road is now traceable in local roads to the city boundary.

Outside the Wheatsheaf pub (now gone) in Chesterton High Street is a fine horse bus, operated by Vinsen's, on its way through the town centre to the railway station in 1910.

Harry Moden lived and worked in Chesterton most of his life. His interest in art fostered his skill as a cartoonist, for which he became locally famous. His cartoons reflected life and events of both Town and Gown. Even today, copies of his postcards are still quite eagerly sought. His business card is illustrated.

The success of Moden's cartoons resulted in several other artists following his example. The card illustrated poked fun at the Cambridge horse tram service, the opinion being, it was said, that it was quicker to walk.

Early postcards, especially those issued by Valentines, offer interesting glimpses of the scene in bygone years. Milton Road in this picture reflects the unhurried ways of the early 1900s. Most of the houses on the left are now shops.

A few yards along Milton Road from the previous picture, town houses faced a large area of open land, then allotment gardens with views to Girton. A snow scene in 1908 included the windmill which stood in open fields that were later to become the Hurst Park estate.

Fen Road, leading to the level crossing and into Chesterton Fen in 1935 was a hedge and tree-lined lane with cornfields behind the hedge and a small narrow field separating it from the river opposite.

Thatched barns flanked Ivy Cottage to the farm in Green End Road – all were destroyed by fire in the early 1950s. The site was cleared and is occupied by council flats.

Sales Nursery was in Arbury Road. Here, in the 1950s, Mr Arbor, the foreman, gathers chrysanthemums.

Sales Nursery staff prepare floral decorations for a college ball in the 1950s.

From Manor Farm in Arbury Road, Mr Cardinal sets out on his milk round in the 1940s.

Maskells bakers in Victoria Road use their new van in 1936 to deliver bread on the Hurst Park estate.

Chesterton Road, Cambridge.

Chesterton Road, here at the boundary with Cambridge town at Chesterton Lane. A Vinsen's horse bus heads towards the town centre, past a row of cottages known to exist as early as 1838.

The horse bus in the last picture is about to pass this brick pier marking the boundary of St Giles Parish and Chesterton Parish.

The privately owned Premier Hall in Union Lane was the venue for many local social events such as weddings, parties and dances. In 1932 it became part of the newly-established Hallens motor business and was converted into showrooms.

A local boys' football team, in the 1930s.

An area in the centre of the village was long known as The Green and at one time had three public houses. Facing is the Maltster's Arms (featured in Chapter Six). On the right is the Haymakers, which still exists, and the Wheatsheaf bears a metal advertisement for the 'Popular Sunday Paper, *The People.*' The date is 1907.

The Maltster's Arms, later the Bleeding Heart, was replaced by a new branch of the Cambridge Co-operative Society at the Green which, in the early 1920s, was the terminus for bus service No. 1, then under the Ortona name.

Hill House (right), in the High Street facing the Green, is one of the most important houses in the village. In earlier days it had attractive and well laid out gardens. Early nineteenth century in brick with an elaborate front door, the house has remained unchanged in appearance for many years, but has suffered from the loss of gardens. It is reputed to be the residence of Edward Fitzgerald while at Cambridge and probably where part of his translation of the Rubyat was done.

At enclosure of the village in 1840, a large parcel of land facing Union Lane and the Green came onto the market. Facing up Union Lane was the property later to become the Haymakers public house, but the outbuildings in this picture taken in the early 1920s were cow sheds.

As Chesterton developed in the 1880s a large block of three-storey houses with basements and attics was built on a commanding site overlooking the river and Jesus Green. It was occupied by college Fellows, local government officials and businessmen. It is now the Arundel Hotel.

At the rear of the houses in the picture above was this range of wooden buildings which were the garage and stables for Vinsen's horse buses. Thoroughly modernised, they are now part of the hotel.

The de Freville estate in the 1880s provided a range of good class houses for the growing population of Chesterton and Cambridge. A healthy situation and easy access to the town with well laid out roads proved very popular.

Humberstone Road on the de Freville estate, c. 1910.

Victoria Road, laid out following village enclosure, was soon lined with Victorian cottages and a selection of shops.

1123g Victoria Park, Cambridge

A view of Victoria Park, a very pleasant cul-de-sac with a central green space, in 1929. Developed in the 1880s – 1890s with semi-detached pairs of good quality town houses, its quiet situation proved popular with local tradesmen and middle range business people.

Although long out of use, a windmill in Hurst Park Avenue still existed beside modern houses in 1930.

Mr Cherry had his shop on the corner of Milton Road and Arbury Road and, for many years, served the increasing number of residents on the estates in the area. This was also the Arbury Road post office. Mr Cherry was a popular figure and, although his general stores closed some time ago, the road junction is still known locally as Cherry's Corner.

Two groups of village gentlemen pose for an historic record of their patronage of the Pike and Eel in the 1880s.

In Chesterton High Street, opposite his home at No. 13, Mr Charles Moule, the local coalman is about to set out on his deliveries.

Union Lane in 1920 and a dustman poses beside his horse and the corporation dustcart.

Parts of Chesterton were isolated from the village centre. Several Cambridge firms had travelling shops to provide household ironware, coconut matting and paraffin oil. Robert C. Brown operated from over the river in Barnwell and is typical of the visitors to outlying houses and farms in the area. This picture dates back to around 1920.

New Chesterton at the end of the nineteenth century was a rapidly expanding area, especially along the Histon and Huntingdon Roads. The need for a new cemetery was met in 1843 when the Cambridge Cemetery Company opened a cemetery in Histon Road for all denominations. Pictured here is the small Tudor-style lodge.

Horace Darwin founded the Cambridge Instrument Company in the 1880s to provide scientific instruments to universities. It went on to become one of the most important firms internationally in its field. Its main works were in Chesterton Road behind the house in this picture (from 1960) after which it was soon to disappear to be replaced by a modern office block for the company.

Typical of the many small shops serving the needs of local people, in both Old and New Chesterton is Sangers on Milton Road. The display of enamel signs was a common sight.

Ted Salisbury started his garage business in the 1930s in a small shed next to the Fleur de Lys in what was then Cam Road. The business prospered and soon crossed the road to be developed as a site with workshops and filling station as seen here in 1965. By 1971, Cam Road had been transformed into a section of the ring road with the new Elizabeth Way bridge, bringing a huge increase in traffic and business.

Petrol filling stations in inner city areas have been closing for many reasons over recent years. Those such as Tom Orbell's on Milton Road, here in 1965, are now only memories.

Until 1939 the University May Week bumping races on the Cam were supported by the Bumps Fair on a meadow in Chesterton Fen opposite Fen Ditton Church. After the war it was never revived. The fair was extremely popular with both town and gown as these 1920s pictures show.

Paying the milkman. A scene in Scotland Road sometime in the 1930s. Four milkmen supplied milk in this way in the village. Unfortunately this particular individual cannot be identified.